LIVING WITH CROHN'S DISEASE

A Story of Survival:

Autobiography by Paul Davies

LIVING WITH CROHN'S DISEASE

A Story of Survival:

Autobiography by Paul Davies

AuthorHouse™
1663 Liberty Drive
Bloomington, IN 47403
www.authorhouse.com
Phone: 1-800-839-8640

First published by AuthorHouse   01/31/2012

ISBN: 978-1-4670-0895-2 (sc)
ISBN: 978-1-4670-0896-9 (ebk)

Printed in the United States of America

Any people depicted in stock imagery provided by Thinkstock are models, and such images are being used for illustrative purposes only.

Certain stock imagery © Thinkstock.

This book is printed on acid-free paper.

Contents

It is 5:15 on 19 December 2009. I pulled on the joint, and I could hear the seeds crackle in the cannabis as it heated up and then turned to ash. My lungs filled with smoke, which leaked into my blood stream and then very quickly spread to my brain, where it clung to receptors. The more I smoked, the more intense the feeling was. My body felt warm and cosy; I closed my eyes for a short moment and imagined I sat in a logged cabin in the Alps. I curled up in the chair in front of a big open fire, and the logs glowed red hot and cracked under the intense heat as the flames jumped and danced as high as they could reach, the heat rising up the chimney and into the cold night air.

As I slowly opened my eyes and came back around, I thought to myself this was the break I needed, but it was against the law. At the time I couldn't understand what all the fuss was about. Looking back, I now understand why marijuana is illegal and a class B drug.

I don't promote the use of cannabis in anyway. It does have a temporary positive side to smoking it, but it also has a lot of negatives to it. The negative side of smoking definitely outweighs the positive side, and I stopped using.

At the age of seven, after eighteen months of sheer hell, I was diagnosed with Crohn's Disease. I'm now thirty-five and ready to tell my story of survival. I have no medical background—I can't even practice first aid—so this autobiography is a firsthand account of the mental and physical torture I have been through. My aim is to try and remove the stigma around the disease. Crohn's Disease is an inflammatory disease which can affect any part of the body, from the mouth to the anus.

Everyone is unique and individual, so the symptoms of Crohn's will vary a lot, from mild to severe. Some Crohn's sufferers can have a flare-up and then go into remission for months or even years. The symptoms I have had to deal with over the years have been severe; I usually have a few good days and then a few bad days. But the older I get, the easier it is to cope.

How does it affect me? I do go to the toilet a few more times than most people, and it can be a little looser, but this is only a very small part of Crohn's. I can be ill without having diarrhoea; this is due to me not being able to eat or drink. Nearly 95 per cent of my diet at the moment is liquid (fort sips). I can go for days without drinking because I'm too ill to do so. If I do try to drink, I can end up heaving. Even water can be difficult to get down, and times like these make me feel so weak.

There are two main things that can make Crohn's a lot worse for me. The first thing is stress and the second is food. But there's a catch: you can't stop stressing or eating. The only thing I can do is to try to not get too stressed and I have changed my diet to a liquid (Fortisip), which is not a cure but does help a lot.

Over the years I have had times where it has gone into remission for a month at a time, but over the past four years for some reason it has never gone away. Some mornings I can't even lift my head up off the pillow—and then I can wake up the next day feeling okay. This has cost me my job, so I am unemployed at the moment.

Over the last couple of years I have tried to get some voluntary work, but as soon as I mentioned I had Crohn's Disease, the door was always slammed in my face. I decided to write my book instead. It will not help you medically, but it might help you realize that you aren't alone.

I have always been strong and a fighter, as well as positive—positivity is a key for me, but it's probably the same for every illness. I'll be honest, it does get hard from time to time, and a year ago I did lose my way and tried to overdose, but now I am back on track and very happy.

Some people may think I'm a parasite on society, sucking the blood out of the system, but please wait till the end before you judge me.

In the Beginning of Space and Time

No one is 100 per cent sure on how or where we have come from. Professors all over the world have suggested that in the beginning there was a big bang, and then space and time popped into existence. I think this is how the universe came to be, and I believe in God, who isn't the same as a person or spirit; he is actually the universe itself. But what has this got to do with me and my book? Well, in the beginning of space and time, there were imperfections, and without these, you and I would have never been. So I do hope if I do make a few mistakes, you remember this paragraph and forgive me, because I'm far from perfect in the English department.

My Personal Crohn's Chart

Cannabis can help all these symptoms.

Fatigue	40%
Pain	40%
Diarrhoea	15%
Being Sick	5%

I've made a basic chart showing the symptoms of the disease and then split each symptom up. I took into consideration how troublesome and how frequent each symptom is. I have put diarrhoea at 15 per cent, which may seem a little low. When the phrase 'inflammatory bowel disease' is mentioned, most people immediately think of the bowel and then diarrhoea, which is right, but the diarrhoea itself is only a small part of Crohn's. I will go into more detail later on how I've made the chart, and how smoking cannabis helped me get through a really bad patch. Then I will discuss why I had to give up something that helped me eliminate my symptoms.

How I Have Organized the Book

Part One

This part starts from when I was born and covers the first flare-up and symptoms of the disease. It goes throughout my school years, till I turned sixteen and left.

Part Two

This section goes into detail about the chart I have made and the symptoms I suffer now or have suffered over the last four years.

Part Three

In this part, I talk about the attempted suicide and why I stopped halfway through. Even now it still sends shivers down my spine, when I think how easy I could have lost my life.

Part Four

In this last part, I discuss how cannabis helped me, and why I decided to stop smoking. There is only one way to explain the effect cannabis had on me. Can you imagine the devil dressed up as a sweet, innocent child? That's how it seemed to me, and I couldn't see him till it was almost too late. Looking back now, one thing I can't believe is how quickly it went from being a medication to being an addiction and the lifestyle than comes with it.

Part One

My Early Life

I was born in 1975. I was a healthy baby with no problems apart from eczema, which started when I was about nine months old. It originated at the back of my ears; from what I can recall as I grew up, the right ear was always a lot better than the left for some reason. They bled and could be very itchy, and then over the years it spread to different parts on my body. I do think I've been lucky over the years; I have seen some children with their hands bandaged up to stop them from scratching. Some children had eczema all over, even on their faces, which looked really painful.

The End of a Virus

'Hello, Mr and Mrs Davies, I am Doctor White.' As I looked up at my parents and the doctors around my cot, all their eyes were focused on me. My sheets were pulled back, and all I had on was a Terrie's nappy. The doctor looked at me and said, 'You poor little man.' The whole of my body was covered in bruises; he tilted his head up so he could talk to my mum and dad and said, 'I know what it is and how to treat it.'

My mum was not too sure about the name of the virus, but the cure was lots of rest, so the doctor said I needed to be in the hospital for a couple of weeks, and I had to stay in my cot for most of the day!

My mum told me how distressing it was for her and my father. Back then hospitals had visiting hours for parents, nine thirty in the morning till seven thirty in the evening. Every morning my mum would wait outside the ward for the doors to be unlocked, so she could see me.

It took me a few weeks to get back on my feet. I was three at this point, and over the next three years, I was healthy except for the eczema. When the time came for me to have my vaccinations, the doctor advised my mum against me having them, due to the eczema. So I was never vaccinated against MMR, and I contracted measles whilst on holiday.

I don't know if it would have made it any worse by having the jabs, but over the next twelve years my eczema got very bad, and it came to a head one afternoon, which really knocked my confidence. I just wanted to hide and never get up again, I was that ashamed. I'll go into more detail later on.

Summer Holiday, 1981

My family and I were driving to Devon for our summer holiday. My parents had chosen a static caravan—I think it was an eight birth. The caravan was on a campsite in Clifford Bridge. After we got off the motorway and drove through the town, we reached the country lanes. The lanes were very narrow, and every couple of minutes my dad had to pull over and let tractors and other cars past, by squeezing the car into the six-foot hedges, which were on either side of the road. After about fifteen more minutes following the signs, we arrived at the campsite.

As my dad drove down the campsite road, we came to a beautiful house and office with a small shop. My dad came out of the office with the keys to the caravan, and we then drove down a path which was about one foot across on either side; it was made from gravel with grass in the middle. I remember there not being very much room in the car. It was a three-door hatch back Nissan Cherry in metallic green. When we got to number eighteen, which was our caravan for the week, my dad reversed the car back and we got out.

There were two doors on the caravan: one single door in the kitchen, which was used all the time, and a double door in the lounge that was never used. I can remember the first few days, but nothing after that. My dad remembered I had contracted measles, and he had to call the local doctor out. When the doctor arrived at the caravan and checked me, he diagnosed me with measles. He told the family to be careful, because it was so contagious. I'm surprised my parents and my sister, Julie, didn't catch it. That would have been a nightmare—the four of us in one caravan, being so sick. My dad said I slept most of the week, and the rest was history.

The First Symptoms of Crohn's

I don't know, and probably will never know, whether the measles kick-started Crohn's. We had only been back from Devon about three weeks when the first symptoms started to flare up. It was really subtle in the beginning, starting off with my stools a little looser than normal. Then I started going to the toilet more than once a day. There wasn't too much pain at the start, but over the next couple of weeks, the stools became softer and more frequent, till eventually it turned into diarrhoea.

Eighteen Months Before Diagnosis

A couple of weeks into the flare-up, the diarrhoea was still persistent, so much so that my mum took me to see the general practitioner. The doctor laid me down on the bed and felt my stomach all over. When he had finished, we sat around his big desk. 'Right, you're constipated, Paul,' he said. That didn't mean much to me at the time. Anyway, the doctor turned his head towards my mum and said, 'What's happed is because Paul's bowel is so bunged up, it's the overflow seeping down into the intestine and coming out as diarrhoea. I'm going to prescribe some laxatives, which will help to soften the stools and make it easier to go to the toilet.'

After we had been to the chemist to get the medication, we drove home. On the way we stopped for some shopping, and I was allowed to choose some sweets, so I decided on Tootie-Fruitis. At the time I didn't know it, but these sweets would eventually feed me and keep me alive for the next year and half, till I was diagnosed with Crohn's Disease.

A few months passed by, and the diarrhoea was still persistent. I think this was when I first started to notice how bad the pain really was. It started in the centre of my stomach before spreading all over. I know this because even now most of the pain I suffer is mainly in the centre. My mum and I went back to see the GP, and he decided to increase the laxatives. He said, 'It will take a while before it starts to work.' Then my mum told him about my loss of appetite, weight loss, pain, and general weakness. He said, 'He'll be fine. When the medicine starts to work, he'll feel a lot better.' He sent us on our way.

A few more months went by, and there was no change—well, the symptoms hadn't changed, but they got a lot worse and started to spiral out of control. The only thing I could eat without being sick was Tootie-Fruitis.

At tea time my mum would call me to come and sit down at the table. As soon as I heard my mum shout, the dread would set in my body. My heart would beat faster and faster as I walked towards the kitchen and smelt dinner. I'd feel nauseated, and some evenings I would be physically sick. I'd sit there forever, just pushing the food around the plate. I did try to eat, but when the food went into my mouth I'd heave; it felt like when one put fingers at the back of one's throat and start gagging. Eventually I'd be allowed to leave the table and go in the lounge.

If I had to pick the tea times I remember the most, it would have to be boil-in-the-bag fish, but for all the wrong reasons. I think it's the source and the little green bits of parsley that did it. The smell of the fish would make my mouth start watering and the sick start flowing. Even now, sitting here writing about it, I feel sick. I never told my mum—it wasn't fair; why should they have to stop eating it because of me? They didn't have it very often, so the dots couldn't be connected for them to realise my aversion.

One evening I was called to the table by my parents. I sat down, and my dad said, 'I have set the buzzer on the oven set for an hour. If you don't eat everything on your plate, you will go straight to bed and won't be allowed your Tootie-Fruiti later in the evening.'

I knew full well that I wouldn't be able to eat my tea; inside I was fuming, and my blood started to boil! I stood up and went ballistic, stamping my feet up and down as hard as I could. I shouted at the top of my voice, 'It's not fair.' The buzzer went off, and he carried out the threat.

The same thing happened the next night, and I got really upset when the buzzer went off. My mum said, 'Before I throw your tea in the bin, are you going to eat it?' I looked at my mum and ran off to my room. About ten minutes later, I heard my dad calling for me to come downstairs.

The next day, about five o'clock, my mum asked me to the table. As I walked towards the kitchen, that same dread set in my body. The smallest taste would make me heave. What was wrong with me? Was I a bad person, being punished? I was screaming inside for someone to help, but no one came!

It was just like most ordinary nights, I thought, so I sat down on the chair, but there was no plate for me. My dad stood up and grabbed the tea towel and pulled my plate from the oven and put it in front of me. My eyes filled up with tears, and then for the first time in the eighteen months before the diagnosis, I collapsed in a heap on the floor and broke down in floods of tears. What they had done was bought a load of Tootie-Fruiti and piled them onto my plate.

An hour or so later, I had calmed down, so my mum made me some warm milk and brought me a digestive biscuit in the lounge. After a few minutes she came to check on me and shouted at the top of her voice for my dad to come quickly. When he came in to the lounge, I was trying to eat the biscuit with a knife and fork. He couldn't take it all in. This was when we knew that something bad was wrong with me, physically and now mentally.

After a year of coming and going to the GP, my mum and I went back to see the doctor, and he got annoyed at us. He said my mum had made me that way by making me in to a mama's boy. He claimed we both needed help, so he sent us to see a psychiatrist. At the time I didn't realise what he had said and where we were going. After a few months the appointment came through the post to go and see the psychiatrist.

Looking back it is difficult trying to remember all the details; I have spoken to my mum about going to see the psychiatrist, and she can't remember much either. She did say that before we went, there was hope and we prayed.

Tootie-Fruiti Diet

Before I go on, I must explain about my diet of sweets. I know how bad that must sound, and I bet you think I should have had a social worker. But for eighteen months, we went to hell and back! All we had was each other. It was only because of my mum's strength that we made it; she never stopped believing that there was actually something wrong with me, which got me through.

All we could do before I'd been diagnosed was live day by day. The portions I was able to eat got smaller and smaller each day. This was a very slow process which went on for months and months, till I couldn't eat any food at all. The only thing I'd be able to put in my mouth without heaving would be something sweet. Even now at thirty-five, I still have problems with food. It's even more of a problem now. Eating to me is more like a chore; I would prefer to put the bins out than have a meal.

When I was first diagnosed with Crohn's; I was prescribed prednisolone as the main treatment. One of the many side effects would be hunger; so the higher the dose, the hungrier I'd be. Some days I found it difficult to satisfy my hunger pains. But over the years my body got used to the effects of the steroids, so there's not the same urge for food anymore.

One thing I remember was when the steroids kicked in for the first time was that my plate was empty. This made my mum smile for the first time in a long time. The spark in her eyes reappeared, and she really enjoyed cooking for me, especially when I ate everything she made.

It's only now, after having my own child, that I can really appreciate how much heart ache my mum went through. I'd like to take this opportunity to say how proud I am of her and how much I love her. I would like to thank her for being there for me.

At the moment 95 per cent of my diet is liquid (Fortisips), and the remaining five per cent is something sweet. If I do eat solid food, I only get pain, so it's not worth it. What I really enjoy is putting Fortisips in the freezer for about forty-five minutes, till it is almost frozen and thick.

Twenty years ago I tried something called Elemental O28. It went well till food was introduced, and then the Crohn's flared up again. I gave it two or three tries, but always the same outcome every time.

The Psychiatrist

When we got to the hospital, we booked in at the reception desk, and the lady behind the desk gave us directions to the waiting room. The nurse on duty weighed and measured me. I can't recollect my height, but my weight was about three and a half stone.

It was quiet in the waiting area; there were only a couple of people in front of us. I went in with my parents, and then I was sent to the waiting area with some paper and crayons. The doctor wanted me to draw what I was thinking. I only remember this because it seemed very strange to me, but I did it.

A while later the nurse called me back into the room, and the doctor said, 'Please sit down and show me your picture.' So I did—it was of me with my mum, dad, and sister. The doctor said, 'That's excellent,' and that made me smile.

'What we have decided is you need to see a consultant in medicine, not a psychiatrist. So we will sort that out straight away.'

Just as we were about to leave, my mum said to the doctor, 'We were planning on going to Scotland for the weekend. Do we cancel or not?'

The doctor took a deep breath and said, 'Let Paul decide, and if he is up to it, then it's okay with me. If for any reason you need medical assistance, go straight to hospital.'

'Thank you, Doctor.'

The Family Weekend in Scotland

I decided that we should go even though I was so weak, I could barely stand up. We left early on Friday morning, and it took a lifetime to get there—well, it seemed that way to a kid. When we arrived at the hotel, it was early in the afternoon, around one o'clock. There was a pair of double doors at the front of the hotel, and as we walked through the doors on the left hand side was the reception area where my dad booked in. We had a family room for Friday, Saturday and Sunday night, then left Monday morning.

On the opposite side of the reception desk was a lounge with tables and comfy chairs. Straight ahead was the bar, and next to that was a shop which sold newspapers, sweets, gifts, and teddies. On the left just before the shop was a door which led to the hotel rooms; our room was on the right, just as we walked through the door.

As soon as we got into the room, I walked to the glass patio window, which opened like double doors, and they were covered all the time with nets. I know my family loved it there, because when I was later diagnosed and in remission, we spent another weekend away there.

We opened the double doors and walked into what felt like a tropical island. The swimming pool was more like a lagoon, and at the edges of the pool the water would barely covered your feet; the further in you walked, the deeper it got. There was a slide and at the bottom you'd shoot out, into the deepest part of the pool.

On the opposite side of the water was a Jacuzzi designed for six adults. Just behind the Jacuzzi were the guest rooms where I slept for most of the weekend, except Sunday afternoon when we all went in the Jacuzzi. A couple of hours before, I had been wrestling with my feet. They felt tight and swollen, the hot water seemed to soothe them. This made me relax and enjoy myself for the first time in a long time. Unfortunately it was not for long though!

When we got out, my mum ran me a bath, and when I was dry and dressed, we went to the restaurant for our tea. My dad persuaded me to have a milkshake. When everyone had finished their meals, I went to stand up, and my ankles were so swollen I couldn't bend my feet. I could feel my eyes starting to fill up with tears, and everywhere looked misty, but through the tears I could see the worried look on my mum's face. My dad put his hands under my arm pits and picked me up. He whispered in my ear, 'don't worry, we will leave tonight and take you straight to the doctor in the morning.' My mum got the suitcases together, and we drove home that evening.

On Monday morning at eight thirty we went to the doctor. In the eighties you had to sit and wait till everyone who was there first had been in to see him, and then it was your turn. There were no appointments like today's system.

We didn't have to wait very long till our turn, and my dad carried me in and put me down on the chair. Some things I remember like yesterday, and this was one of those times. The doctor looked at me and then at my mum and dad, and he said, 'What do you want now? I thought I told you not to come back.' He was really abrupt with us.

This got my dad very mad—I don't blame him, though; I'd be the same if it was Chloe, my daughter. He looked at the physician and said, 'Look at his feet and ankles.'

The doctor's jaw hit the desk. 'Oh my God, they are swollen!' He started writing and talking at the same time, and then he put the letter in an envelope and handed it to my father. He said 'I think Paul may have cancer. I want you to go straight to Pendlebury Children's Hospital; head to A and E and hand this letter to the doctor on duty.'

From seeing a shrink to being told I may have cancer was a bit of a shock. I'll give him credit, though: he went to apologise to my parents—or maybe was he just covering his own back; we will never know. I don't hold any grudges against the doctor. He wasn't very old, and he may have not even known anything about Crohn's at that point in his career. I hold no grudges; I think if one does, it turns into bitterness, and I don't want that.

When we got to hospital, we went straight to A and E. We didn't have to wait very long till a bed on the chemo ward was made available for me. I remember walking down the ward with a nurse to my bed, and I was shocked to see all the sick children, wired up to all sorts of machines; most of them had lost their hair. The thing I remember the most was how happy they looked, even though they were going through hell. I think children are more resilient than most people give them credit for.

The first few days were hard, especially at night when my mum and dad had gone home; I guess I was homesick. I was only eight at the time and thought I was going to die any day, never to see them again. The sicker I got, the more I thought about the reason I was sent to the hospital by the doctor. My conclusion was that I was there to die!

I had never spoken to anyone about how I felt, not even to my mum or dad. Even now I find in difficult to talk to anyone; over the years I have seen many counsellors, who haven't helped very much. The only thing which has is writing; I find it therapeutic.

Over the two-week period before I was transferred to Booth Hall Children's Hospital, I had a lot of tests done. The more invasive procedures where done in the operation theatre: a barium meal, a barium enema, and an endoscope.

My last test was at a different hospital, and I was there all day. It was Friday afternoon when I got back to Pendlebury.

On Monday afternoon a consultant from Booth Hall Children's Hospital came to see me. Dr Evens was a very quiet, compassionate, and kind man. He asked lots of questions and felt my stomach, and then he sat down next to my mum and said to her, 'I've looked at all the tests results and have a diagnosis for Paul: he has Crohn's Disease.'

My mum's eyes filled with teas and asked, 'How long has he got left?'

He smiled and then held my mum's hand. 'A long time; it's a bowel disease. It can't be cured, but we can treat it. The treatment will be a high dose of prednisolone, which is a steroid.' He explained all about the disease and how much better I'd feel. I was very sceptical at this point and didn't think I would ever get better due to me being so ill and underweight. 'We will move Paul to Booth Hall and start the treatment today; he will be under my care. Is that okay with you and Paul?'

'Yes, thank you, Doctor.'

When Dr Evens had gone, my mum put her arms around me and started to cry, which set me of. She said to me, 'You are not going to die,' and we just hugged each other as hard as we could. Then she said, 'I'm going to phone Dad and tell him the good news,' and off she went. A few minutes later my dad came strolling down the ward and said, 'Where's Mum?'

I said, 'She has gone to phone you to tell you the good news: I'm not dying.' My dad didn't really know what to make of what I had said. A minute or so later my mum came back and told him all about what the doctor had said.

I was transferred by an ambulance that afternoon to Booth Hall. My mum and dad didn't know how to get to the hospital, so they followed behind in their car. When we arrived we were taken straight upstairs to ward nineteen. The staff started the medication straight away. I'm not 100 per cent sure, but I think the dose of prednisolone was eighty milligrams.

After a week I felt a lot better, so Dr Evens said I could go home. I was only home for a few days when my face swelled up. We went back to the ward, and Dr Evens came down to see me and said the steroids that I was on held onto the water in my body, making me puff up. 'The only thing you can do is to try to cut down on your salt intake.' That was easier said than done. I remember going to a Burger Bar with my mum and sister, and I asked for some chips without salt. The girl behind the counter huffed and said, 'I'll have to make more fries, then, and you will have to wait.' My mum said that was okay, and the girl looked annoyed as she turned around to make them.

After two weeks I went back to school, and when I got to the playground every kid in the school stared at me. The reason was because the last time I'd been to school, I was so skinny, and now I was back like the Michelin man. My new nickname was fish, and it stuck till I left at sixteen.

At dinner I went from eating nothing to eating everything. In my lunch box was two barm cakes, two packets of salt, and shake crisps without the salt. I had to open both packs and put them into a plastic bag, so no one knew I had two bags; this would have given the kids even more reason to tease me!

At the time I didn't know what side effects were, but I felt the full force of them. I know I have mentioned this before, but I was so hungry all the time, and I'd wake up in the middle of the night and go downstairs for something to eat. Even eating through the night didn't fill me up—it was horrible. This went on till the prednisolone was reduced, but then the Crohn's would flare up, and the steroids were increased again.

<u>Moving to Secondary School</u>

In between being diagnosed at eight and leaving junior school, I missed months of schooling during this period, so at the age of eleven I couldn't read or write. My first day at secondary school was horrible. All the new kids had to go to the hall and sit on chairs. We had to wait till our name was called out in alphabetically order. When they had finished calling all the names, there were about fourteen of us left. 'Right, everyone who is left, you are all in the bottom set, and you will be known as the remedial class, so follow me.'

Shit. As if I wasn't bullied enough! This would give the kids so much more ammo.

The classroom I was in was a portacabin on the other side of the school. It felt like a special classroom for the idiots, especially with the room being separated from the rest of the school. When we got to the cabin and sat down, we had to introduce ourselves to each other. Then the teacher said to all of us, 'If it wasn't for my kind-hearted self, you would all be in a special school. When you leave at sixteen, none of you will get jobs.' I couldn't believe how negative he was with us. I felt like giving up before I'd even started.

I'm going to jump to when I was eighteen for a minute. At this point in my life I'd been working for two years and passed my driving test. I had my own car, and one afternoon after I'd finished work, I was driving home in the rain past my old school and spotted the teacher, who had told me I was a waste of time. He was walking toward the bus stop in the rain. I laughed all the way home.

Growing up as a Teenager

There's one piece of advice I would give: do not tell anyone of school age that you have Crohn's Disease, because it might cause you hell. I'd been very fortunate; when I was a teenager, not many people knew about Crohn's and what it was. Everyone at school knew I was ill but didn't know why. If they did, I think things would have probably been worse, and I would have not gone in. When I left school I had no qualifications, but that didn't matter at the time—I was just glad to leave.

Growing up as a teenager was hard, especially with a big dark secret like mine. I would rather have died than let anyone know.

Being on a high dose of steroids had its highs and lows. One day I could be so happy, but the next day I'd be really sad and angry. I went through a stage of having fights and arguing with anyone and everyone. Some of it was due to puberty and just growing up, but the medication didn't help with the emotional side, and I was trying to cope with being ill, making it even harder to get through.

When I was about thirteen, I tried to reduce the high dose of steroids, but every time I did the Crohn's just flared up. The doctor decided to try Elemental O28; I don't know if this is still used today or not. It is a liquid diet which my mum and dad made fresh every day. They would use cold-boiled water and put the water into a big jug with the powder and mix it all together. Then they divided the liquid into separate bottles, leaving just enough in the jug to fill three to four ice cube trays and freeze them. They placed the bottles in the fridge.

When it was time to drink one, I placed seven or eight ice cubes in a pint pot and smashed them up. Then I poured one bottle from over the top and drank it. The colder the drink was, the more palatable it was to drink. After a couple of weeks, I grew to like it. Apart from being hungry all the time, it worked quite well. But when I tried to introduced solid food slowly, the symptoms started to flare up again. Over the next year or two I tried twice more, and every time the conclusion was the same.

My First Operation

Things got bad when I was around fifteen, and I was rushed into the hospital. I was underweight; the pain was horrendous, and I was very weak. The doctor ordered the same tests as I had when I was first diagnosed. The only test I didn't have was the special test at the other hospital. When all the results came back, it didn't look good: there were a lot of narrow parts in my bowel, and it was very inflamed. When the doctor did his morning round, he came armed with a plan of action. The first thing he wanted was to build me up with liquid food intravenously for a month; he wanted me to be as well built up as I could be before the operation. Then I could be operated on, to remove the narrow parts and some of the inflamed pieces of my intestine. This would give me the best chance of recovery.

After the surgery I'd have to stay on the surgical unit for about twelve days. I couldn't believe my luck—six weeks stuck in hospital. I got really defensive and said, 'No! I can't stay in here for that long.'

Dr Evens looked at me, and then he scratched his head and said, 'Okay, what about going home for a few hours on Saturday morning, and coming back in the evening? You can do the same on Sunday, up until the operation date. Is that okay?' I took his compromise.

On Monday afternoon, the staff set up and started the intravenous machine. The drip stand had a box on it, I think to detect air bubbles and prevent them going into the blood stream. The annoying thing was the alarm it had, especially at night—it went off all the time to warn the nurses that there was a problem.

The ward I was on had individual rooms with one, two, or three beds. I had a two-bed room, and over the weeks the bed opposite me had a lot of different children coming and going. I was the oldest on the ward; I think the oldest patient that stayed in my room was about ten. There was a playroom on the ward, but all the toys were for younger children, and I got very bored.

The ward next to mine had a room that both wards used for school. Every morning when I spotted the teacher coming to collect all the children, I would try and hide or pretend to be asleep. But one morning she came around early and caught me off-guard.

'Morning, is it, Paul?'

'Yes,' I said.

'I know you're fifteen, and we don't usually teach older teenagers, but you're welcome to join us. I can probably find something for you to do on the computer.'

I thought for a second and said, 'Yes, please.' To my surprise I really enjoyed it. The computers were very basic compared to today's, but they were modern for the time.

As I sat using the computer, I could hear one of the children, a boy about nine or ten, having a real good whine at the teacher, trying to get out of the schoolwork he had been assigned. I thought I was good, but this lad went one better. He had his elbows on the desk, both hands on each side of his face, and his back bent over. I could almost see his brain ticking, and then all of a sudden he must have had a eureka moment. His back went straight, his head raised high, and then he made eye contact with the teacher and said, 'Miss, I feel really sick.'

She looked at him and said, 'That's why you're in hospital. Now, get on with your work.'

Then he collapsed back down into his chair; this act brought a smile to my face.

It was about a week and a half till my operation. On Sunday evening my mum and dad had just taken me back to the ward. I'd only been there for a minute when I was hooked back up to my machine. I didn't mind, though, because my favourite nurse did it. She must have been about twenty-five and gorgeous; at the time I thought I was in love, but it was more like a teenage crush.

I was so tired when I got to bed that night I dropped off straight away. About three in the morning I woke up with a stinging pain in my arm, and the nurse on duty that night gave me something for the pain so that I could go back to sleep. About an hour later the pain got so bad that the doctor had to be called out. When he arrived he felt the vein and checked up and down my arm. He said, 'The vein had collapsed due to the amount of fluid going through it.'

At half past four in the morning, they swapped arms. The sore arm had to be strapped with something like a splint, and then they put a bandage round it to keep it straight. When the doctor had finished, he said to me, 'Would you like something for the pain?'

'Yes, please.'

'Okay then, Paul, I'm going to give you an injection in your bottom. This will help with the pain, and it might make you a little bit sleepy. So can you stay in bed for me, please?'

'Yes, Dr.'

(As I sit here writing, my daughter Chloe has just said to me, 'How can you remember everything that happened to you in the past?' The reason is that this five-week period was such a traumatic time in my life. There are two things that really stand out, which I haven't gone into yet, but I will later. It doesn't really affect me now, but back then it had a devastating effect on me as a teenager.)

The next few days went okay till about Friday, when the other vein collapsed. This was the last straw, and I took control for the first time in my life. Till this point my mum had done all the talking for me, and I had laid back and let her.

When the doctor came round with the nurse, I told them I couldn't take much more and decided that the treatment had to stop. They agreed with me and stopped the treatment straight away; it was due to stop on Sunday anyway. But the damage had been done by now, and my arms were in agony. Both arms were now strapped and out of action, and it left me really depressed. The nurses kept the pain under control, but I had to stay in hospital for the weekend. By this time

I was so pissed off that I didn't want to get out of bed anyway. I thought things couldn't get any worse, but this was just the start.

Monday morning came round pretty quick, and the surgeon came to see me first thing and went through everything they were going to do. It didn't sound very nice, but it had to be done. One of the doctors said to me, 'You will have to have your bowel washed out. What will happen is a very small, flexible tube will be put in your bottom, and warm water will go down the tube and into your tummy, and then it will be drained back out. I said that was okay, thinking I'd be asleep when it happened. Boy, was I wrong.

They started me on another drug, to help wash the bowel out before my operation. I had to drink it which was not very nice, and then over the next few hours I had to drink as much water as I could. It worked very quickly—I was on the toilet all afternoon and evening with a lot of pain. Eventually the pain and diarrhoea stopped, and I must have fallen asleep.

When I got up on Tuesday morning, all I could have to drink was water, and I couldn't have anything to eat till about six days after surgery. Around one thirty the nurse that I had fallen for came on duty; I will call her Katy because I can't remember her name. She came to check my temperature and blood pressure and made sure I was okay.

About three o'clock Katy came back and said, 'Right, Paul you have to come with me to the treatment room, to be washed out.' My heart missed a beat, and then that feeling of complete dread went through my body; I was so scared. The only thing I kept thinking was at least she didn't know my secret, so I got up and went to the treatment room with her. It was worse than I could possibly have imagined. When I got into the room, I had to lie down with my back to her. It didn't hurt; it was the smell more than anything. It was like going to the toilet in front of her, and all my dignity went out of the window.

This had a lasting effect on me. The only toilet I will go on is my own; if I'm not well, I will not risk going out just in case. My mum and dad came round the other day, and I needed to go but had to wait till they had gone. If I've been to the toilet, and someone comes round, I'll hide and not let them in. It takes a few hours before I am commutable enough to let someone in my flat. I have to flush the toilet two to three times, to get the water clear. I can't imagine what the neighbours must think.

When it was over, I ran back to my bed and jumped into it. All I wanted to do was hide forever and not get up. A while later Katy came to cheek on me; she wasn't stupid and knew how mortified I was. But she was so professional and made me feel like it wasn't a problem. As Katy left the room, I smiled at her.

The next morning, my mum was able to come first thing so she could be there when the doctors did their ward rounds and go over any last-minute questions before the big day. There were a couple of things that I needed to ask, just too put my mind at ease. One thing that worried me was waking up on the operating table. I had been put to sleep before for medical reasons, when I was very young, but I had no recollection of having it done. They assured me things like that didn't happen, and they would monitor me all the way through the operation. This put me at ease, but I was still scared.

When the doctors had been to see me, my mum walked out with them and must have told them how bad my eczema had been.

At dinner time my mum went home for a few hours. She said she'd come back later in the day with my dad. As soon as my mum had gone, I started to get stressed about the last bowel washout coming up that afternoon. I've never spoken to anyone about it till now—things like that should be left in the past; but writing it down and getting it off my chest has done me a world of good.

An hour or two later, Katy came to see if I was okay and said, 'Can you come to the treatment room with me?'

The dread set in my body as soon as the words hit my ears, and I froze on the spot for a second, which felt like a lifetime. Eventually I got off my bed and said, 'Okay.'

As we walked down to the room, Katy said, 'Don't worry, it's a swab which the doctor is going to be doing. Someone else will be doing your bowel washout later this afternoon.'

'Oh, right,' I said, and then I realised what she meant. Shit, what could I do? The first thing I thought was to turn around and run; not the best idea I ever had, but it could have worked. The only other idea was to collapse, but this may have jeopardised the surgery in the morning, so that was a bad idea too. As we got closer and closer to the door of the treatment room, my legs started shaking, and my stomach turned like a washing machine on the spin cycle. The inside of my body was screaming, 'You freak, you bloody freak.' Then everything seemed to slow down as Katy reached for the handle to open the door. The emotions rushing through my mind were unbelievable. I didn't know whether to laugh or cry. My forehead started to sweat, as she opened the door.

When I got in to the treatment room, the doctor asked me to pull my shorts down so he could take a sample. By this point my eyes had started to fill up as I pulled my pants down. The look on both their faces was one of shock; all they said was, 'Ouch, that looks sore.' As I pulled my penis up for the doctor, the skin split open at the base where the top of the scrotum joined. It was all bloody with fresh blood and blood that had dried and gone black. The shaft of my penis was red and raw, and at the end where the bell bit was, there were little red ulcers all over, starting to bleed. It looked like it had gangrene and was starting to decay. As I looked down at it, all I wanted to do was get hold of it and rip it off. This caused me so many traumas over the years. Even now it comes and goes, but now I have learnt to deal with it and don't think that way.

As soon as the procedure had been done, I walk back to my bed and broke down in tears. I didn't have much luck up till now, but the bed on the opposite side of mine was empty for the first time, so I was by myself. The nurse came to check on me about five minutes later, and even though I was mortified, she made me feel better by talking to me and assuring me that they could treat it with cream.

Looking back now, as I walked down the corridor to the treatment room, I think the thing that worried me the most was the fear of being laughed at by the doctor and the nurse—which they didn't. I think this paranoia came from being bullied at school.

Just before Katy went off-duty, she came to wish me good look for my operation, because she had a few days off, and I'd be on the surgical ward after my surgery, so I would never see her again. I don't remember very much after that, till I woke up after the operation.

After the Operation

'Paul, Paul, it's Mum. Are you okay? It's all over now; everything went according to plan with no complications.' I slowly opened my eyes to make eye contact with my mum, but the room spun, and I felt really spaced out and closed my eyes again. My mum spoke to me again. 'Paul, they did the operation, and you didn't need a colostomy bag.' This got my attention, and the relief was so welcoming.

There was only me and mum who knew how worried I was about having a colostomy bag. The reason behind this was that it smelled so bad when I went to the toilet. I would have died if it came in public and someone had got a whiff of it. This would have destroyed me and my confidence. One day I might have to have one, and now that I'm older it would be a lot easier to handle.

It took till dinner time the next day before I came round, and then the pain felt quite intense. I had a tube up my nose and down my throat into my stomach, so the acid could be drawn up. There were drips and all the other bits as well. They controlled the pain well, so that wasn't a problem. It was not being able to drink that was the killer; my mouth was so dry. The only thing I could have was a damp piece of gauze, which was hell; it felt like I was being teased. All I wanted to do was squeeze all the water out, but it was too dry to do that.

It must have been about five days till my bowel started to work again. I remember the nurse came over after the doctors had been to see me, and she said 'You are allowed to have a small drink now. I will go and get it for you.' I think psychologically, not being able to have something that I wanted made the need for it a lot more intense.

The nurse came over five minutes later and handed me a plastic medicine cup, it must have contained only twenty-five millilitres of orange juice in it; at first I thought it was medication. 'There you go, Paul,' said the nurse as she handed it over to me.

I looked at her and said, 'What is it?'

'It's the drink I said you could have.'

'You're winding me, up aren't you?'

'No. And drink it slow; it has to last you for an hour. If you're not sick, you can have some more.'

There wasn't much there, but it felt good just to have a moist mouth. Over the next several hours I was allowed more and more till I was drinking freely.

The next day after the doctors had been round, they authorized the nurses to take out all the tubes. What a relief when the tube from my nose came out, though it didn't taste very nice when it passed the back of my throat.

I started to count the days till I could go home. As I sat on my bed, I could see my mum and a couple of my friends, Simon and Peter, walking towards the bed. My mom said, 'Right, Paul, I am going to leave you to it for hour, and then I'll take Simon and Peter home'.

It was good to see my mate's, because I hadn't seen them for weeks. When they left, I had a sleep and was woken up at tea time by the nurse. She said, 'You can have some tea tonight. It's mashed potato, and jelly for afters.' Lucky me, I thought. The mash looked like wallpaper paste and smelt awful. I didn't dare taste it, so I tried the jelly, which was okay.

After a few days I was allowed to go home; it felt a little strange at first, but I soon got back in to the swing of things. But after a few months the pain and diarrhoea started all over again. I couldn't believe it. I had to be rushed back into hospital for more surgery. The good thing this time was that I didn't have to be built up, because there was no time—they had to operate straight away.

After My Second Surgery

After the second surgery, things started to settle down, and I felt better than I had in a long time. I was almost sixteen and in the last year of school. One thing that stood out at school was PE and games.

Even though I had picked up a lot, I still had ulcers and scabs all over my penis, which still resembled gangrene. The cream which had been prescribed for me by the doctor helped but didn't eliminate the problem. I was so scared that the class might see it in the shower at school. After PE and games, we had to have a shower, especially in the winter months; we could get really muddy after playing football or rugby. During my first week back to school, I was petrified on the day I had games. I didn't want to tell my mum about how I felt; she'd seen me go through so much already. I kept it to myself for the time being. The only way I could get out of doing games was to have a note from my mum, saying I had Crohn's Disease and was not well enough to do it. But the PE teacher I had didn't like me, and I didn't like him. He thought it was all to do with me not being athletic, which got him really annoyed. I preferred he didn't know.

At eleven thirty I walked into the PE department, and the teacher said, 'Hello, how are you doing after your operation?'

'Okay, thank you.'

He knew I'd been poorly but didn't know anything about why I'd had surgery. Then I told him I'd forgotten my football kit, to get out of doing it. His whole demeanour changed towards me, and in a stern voice he said, 'Go and get something from the lost property box.' I grumbled at him and walked off.

Games were eleven thirty till dinner time, at twelve thirty, so I decided to go home without telling him and have an early dinner. In the afternoon he caught up with me and went mad. He said, 'I've been looking for you for most of the lesson, when I should have been out teaching on the field.' I told him I had felt sick and went home, and then after dinner I started to feel better, so I decided to come back. He calmed down and said, 'If you ever do that again without telling someone, you're in serious trouble.' He let me off with a warning.

When I got to school in the morning, the teachers took the register, and then every lesson throughout the day each teacher would take his or her own register. So the week after, when I had games, I didn't let the teacher see me and went home at eleven thirty. He presumed I had been off all day, and I must have been ill. This worked for a few weeks, till one afternoon when he spotted me going from one lesson to the other. It was like a bomb going off. 'Where the hell were you this morning? I thought you were ill.' Then he dragged down to see the head of year.

We went into the office, and the head of year sat behind his desk. He said, 'Please sit down,' and before he could say anything, the games teacher started shouting at me. He was like a big kid who had spat his dummy out. I couldn't understand it; it was if PE was the most important lesson in school. When he had calmed down, they decided to give me a detention and said they were going to keep an eye on me.

A week later, when the bell went for the next lesson, I couldn't believe the PE teacher was outside the room, waiting for me. He escorted me to the changing room for games. He had the biggest smile I had ever seen. 'Come on then, Davies, get changed.' He never called me Paul—it was always Davies. He had no respect for me, so I didn't respect him. He said it again: 'Get ready, Davies.'

I thought, Shit, what do I do? I did the only thing I could think of. I told him, 'No.'

That didn't go down well. 'If you don't, there will be trouble.' I told him the first thing that came into my head, which was I had forgotten my kit. 'Well, you know what to do then, don't you?'

I looked at him and said, 'No, sir.'

'Go and get something out of the lost property box.' I panicked and didn't know what say, so I decided to tell him I was too ill and couldn't do games. He got really annoyed at me, and then when everyone had gone outside to the football field, he told me to stay in the changing room, and then he closed the door and locked me in. It wouldn't have bothered me very much, but because I was on a high dose of steroids, I really lost it.

Being on a high dose of steroids can really help to control the Crohn's, but some of the side effects were really hard to deal with, especially on the emotional side. The feelings I could go through were unreal. For me there were three sets of emotions. The first emotion I suffered with over the years was the worst of all three. It came on as quick as a click of the fingers, and my mood changed from being calm and relaxed to being teary and very sad. Then it would go just as quick as it had come. When I was younger I didn't talk to anyone about it, but now that I'm older I can, and doctors prescribed me Fluoxetine, which helps.

The second side effect came as quickly as the first and was just as intense. To be honest, there was not much difference between them; they were both hard to deal with. This second effect made me feel like *crap*. I would get very restless and twitchy, and then really angry. It almost felt like I was going to pop, there was so much hate and rage inside. Like the first side effect, it went as quick as it came.

The third and final emotion was the nice side to being on steroids. This too could come and go instantly. It was the feeling of exhilaration, which could make me feel really excited and invincible; the effect was even stronger when I was younger. I think some young adults believe they are invincible, and being on steroids magnified the situation a lot more.

I'd been locked in the changing room, and at the time my dose of steroids was very high, and the raging mood swing came over me. I walked over to the door and tried opening it with my key, but it wouldn't fit. I went over to the windows, and the windows that were accessible were locked. With every second that went by, I became more stressed. I walked back over to the door, which was made from solid wood with no glass in it. I started banging and kicking it. Then I thought to myself, there is no way out—if the school is set on fire I am trapped and will be killed.

As I kicked the door and shouted at the top of my voice, I heard a key turning in the lock; it was the games teacher. Somebody had been out onto the field and told him that someone was trying to kick the door down in the changing room. The door swung open, and he flew through it and got hold of me at the top of my neck were my tie was. He pushed me against the wall, shouting at the top of his voice. I managed to break free and ran off. As I ran down the corridor, I turned and said, 'Just you wait till my dad hears about this—you're deed!' Then I went home.

My mum and dad went into school that afternoon to sort things out with the head of year. I decided that they could tell him about Crohn's Disease, as long as he didn't tell anyone else what I had. Between them they decided I could go to the library instead of doing games.

I never told my dad what I'd said to the teacher, that he would beat him up. My father was not a fighter; he was gentle and didn't like trouble. It probably got the games teacher a little worried, though.

Between Sixteen and Thirty

I left school at sixteen with no qualifications, but despite all of that I found a job and worked for about fifteen years, before I become too ill to continue.

When I was in my early twenties, I started seeing a girl who lived near my mum. We'd only been together a year before my daughter was born. Eighteen months later we got married, but it didn't work, and we ended up getting divorced when I was thirty. I don't think it's fair to go into any details; one thing I can say, though: it may have worked if I didn't have Crohn's. We get along better now, being divorced. I think that's important when children are involved.

The Good and the Not So Good

The Side Effects of Steroids (Prednisolone) on My Body

Over the years the use of steroids, specifically prednisolone, took its toll on my bones. I now suffer with osteoporosis, which resulted in my left hip having to be replaced a few years ago. In my opinion it's worth it; I'd rather have weak bones and keep the Crohn's under control.

I have taken thousands of steroids over the last twenty-seven years. From what I can remember, I have never had any bad infections while being on a higher dose of prednisolone, though it can happen.

In the beginning when the Crohn's first flared up, the consultant put me on a very high dose of prednisolone, and then he brought them down fast. He thought it was the best way to treat the disease, rather than having to keep increasing the tablets slowly, till the disease went into remission.

The first few weeks I felt like a superhero, and my energy level went from 0 to 100 per cent. I was ready to take on the world. Then after a couple more weeks, the bad side of the steroids reared its ugly head. The first thing I noticed was a lack of concentration, while trying to relax or watch TV or build something with my LEGOs. I couldn't sit for more than five minutes without fidgeting and getting very angry. Going to bed started to stress me out, and trying to relax was impossible. Some nights I'd lie awake tossing and turning, and then I'd be nodding off during the day.

One minute I was happy and felt good inside—and then the next minute my mood changed to anger, and my body felt like it was going to explode. When this happened I felt like smashing things up. Even though I was so angry inside, I never did anything too stupid. When I got that bad, the only way to keep it together was to have a real good cry. The relief felt so good inside, it was like someone had lifted a huge weight off my shoulders.

There were some positives to the steroids: they controlled the pain and diarrhoea. When the dose was high enough, I could eat very small amounts of food, but to be honest I'd rather not. The mood swings that I had settled down when my body got used to the higher dose of prednisolone. I could live with the side effects; it was all about getting the balance right. I thought quality of life outweighed the quantity.

The Quirky Things I've Done over the Years

I have certainly done many quirky thing in my life. One time I was about nineteen. I had my own car and was with my mate, we pulled up to see a couple of girls we knew. We got out to chat to them. As I stood talking, my stomach started churning, I had to clinch my bum cheeks, trying to stop the diarrhoea from coming out. After a minute or two it settled down, and I thought, Wow, that was close. Then the smell came.

It must have only been a teaspoonful, but it stunk to high heaven; I was mortified and jumped in my car and drove home as fast as I could. This was the first and only time something like that had ever happened. When I got home I flew up the stairs to the bathroom, stripped, and jumped into the shower.

This got me thing about Katy the nurse and the day she washed my bowel out for surgery. The situation was different, but the outcome was still the same—I was mortified. This time I had been pushed too far, so over the next few years, I was so paranoid about the smell, each time I went to the toilet I'd get undressed; even my socks came off, because I was so scared that I'd get diarrhoea on any of my cloths.

When I finished on the toilet, I would wash the whole of my body. Or if there was time, I'd have a shower. Then I would check my body all over to make sure I was clean.

After this one accident, I stayed in the house for a few days before going out again. Nobody said anything to me; even so, my confidence took a huge knock.

Another thing that I have done in the past is if I needed to go to the toilet at work, I would wait till dinner time and go home. Some days I could be doubled up in pain, but I wouldn't dare go just in case someone came into the toilet and smelt it. It would take me ten minutes to get out of the building, and drive home. When I got home I'd run to the bathroom, go to the toilet, and then have a wash—all in ten minutes. Then I drove back to work, which would take me another ten minutes. This usually happened ever day. I don't work now due to bad health, so it's not a problem anymore.

If I've been to the toilet recently and someone comes knocking on the door, I will hide till they've gone. I'll do this for about two to three hours, till I think the smell has gone. Chloe is the only person I allow in my flat while I go to the toilet.

Between the age of about seventeen and my last operation, which I haven't talked about, I was very skinny and weighed seven stone. People used to think I was anorexic, and this really got to me I hated being thin and wished I could have been bigger with muscles. I've gone the other way now—I have a big stomach and weigh about eleven stone.

Part Two

Symptoms of Crohn's

Fatigue: 40%

Fatigue: is the main part of Crohn's Disease. It feels like the heart is slowing down with every beat.

Some mornings when I wake up, I will open my eyes very slowly, and my vision will be bleary as everything around me spins. It feels like my body has been run over by a steam roller. The only way to compare it is to having the flu. My whole body will be shaking and gets very hot and sweaty, and then I'll shiver and feel cold and wet. If I try to get out of bed, I will feel dizzy and flop back down. If Chloe is in she will help me and makes sure I'm okay before she goes out. If I'm by myself and do need something, I have to crawl around on my hands and knees, so I'm able to get where I need to go.

Usually if I have to get up, it's for medication, which I need to obtain from the kitchen. The other thing I always need is bath towels, which I place on the bed. I have to do this quite often to help soak up the sweat from my body. The sweating only started about four years ago, and it's now one of the main symptoms from which I suffer.

On days like this, I may only go to the toilet once or twice a day with diarrhoea. This is probably due to the lack of liquid inside my body. Trying to drink my Fortisips isn't easy; I end up heaving because they're quite thick and hard to get down. When I feel well there lovely, especially in the summer when they've been in the freezer. Water is just as hard, so I have little sips through the day.

Then some days I feel okay but have no energy to do anything; I usually end up staying in bed and sleeping all day. On days like this it feels like it's a waste of a life, just lying there. On a good day I'll use every second to the fullest.

Pain: 40%

Physical Pain

The physical pain covers quite a large area, anywhere from my mouth to my bottom, and it can vary from mild to severe. Some days I can wake up feeling really poorly, and my stomach can churn and is full of wind. It's okay if I'm by myself, but when Chloe's at home, it's not nice for her, and it's embarrassing for me.

Sometimes my stomach can feel really hard, and I find it difficult to go to the toilet. Having a hot bath can help, but when I get out the pain comes back.

Sometimes it feels like a million maggots eating away my bowel; more likely than not, I end up rolling about in severe pain. I also sweat buckets, which soaks whatever I'm wearing and all the bed sheets. When the pain and the feeling of being unwell has subsided, the sweat and smell disappear.

The worst pain is in my back passage and bottom. The pain is horrendous; I will walk around my flat, trying to get away from my body and the pain. It never works, though. It can get so bad that I have tears in my eyes and find it hard not to overdose accidently on pain meds. I have put a kitchen knife to my wrist and almost did it on a few occasions. The reason I don't do it is because I love my daughter a lot more than the pain that hurts me.

I really love life and would like to stay alive as long as I can, especially for Chloe. I'd like to see her become an adult and settle down with her own family.

A lot of the time the pain that I suffer is debilitating, and it frequently affects my life in a big way because it can keep me in bed for days at a time.

Mental Pain

There's also the mental pain that I suffer. I don't think its depression; it's more being sad and unhappy when I'm not well. I've mentioned about running away from my body, which is impossible. The only other way is to be dead—it is an option, but I don't want to die—so the thing that gets me through is knowing that things will settle down, and I will have good days in between the bad days.

I have now been single for six years, so on the bad days it doesn't matter if I sweat and feel dirty. Don't get me wrong, I do hate it, but no one has to see or smell me.

It doesn't matter how old I get; it still hurts that some people will take me at face value, so I don't have a chance for them to see through the disease and inside to my soul.

I'll stay in if I'm feeling poorly and will not go anywhere, unless it's to the hospital. On the good days I do like to get out, even if it is only around the corner to the shops for a bit.

When people who know me see me out and about, they don't know if I'm well or not on that particular day. I often wonder what they're thinking to themselves, especially if they are behind me in a queue in a local shop. I don't know but I bet they're often scared, in case I have an accident next to them. I can just imagine when I've gone out of the shop, and the person standing behind me has their turn at the till. The shop assistant goes to give him or her change, but the person will refuse it, just in case I had my dirty, contagious fingers all over the money and contaminated it. Things do happen, but it's only very rarely that someone will actually go too far and hurt me.

If you're reading my story and you have just been diagnosed with Crohn's Disease or something similar, just remember there are also a lot of nice people out there to. If you do come across anyone nasty, they are the ones with the problem, not you.

I know that throughout my book, I keep going over the same thing time and time again, but it's very important to keep positive. Just tell yourself that the good days will come, so grab them with both hands and enjoy them the best you can.

Diarrhoea: 15%

I can go for months without having severe diarrhoea, and then it can hit me very hard without warning. Some nights I can be up all night with accidents, having to get in the bath to wash myself. Some days I get really tired, and can have accidents in the daytime as well as night.

It's not always like water, but for some reason it's never formed when I go to the toilet. It could be all the surgery or my liquid diet, I'm not sure. One thing I've never suffered is mucus, and very rarely there might be a spot of blood, but nothing to complain about. Now that I don't go to work, I don't have to leave my flat if I'm not well, so if I do have severe diarrhoea, I'm always near the bathroom.

Being Sick: 5%

It's almost pointless putting being sick on the chart, because I rarely get sick. In my opinion, being physically sick and just feeling sick are two different things. The Crohn's has to be severe for me to be sick, so if I stay in bed, I'm okay. It's only if I move about that I feel dizzy. If I'm in bed and get up, I'll move slowly, which helps.

Part Three

The Suicide Attempt

It was about six months before 12 December 2009. Even though I was starting to become very unwell, I was still having some good days. I decided to look into doing some voluntary work to keep myself busy. So I got a curriculum vitae together, and my mum drove me round, to the house of a couple that ran a charity.

I knocked on the door, and a well-dressed lady answered. I said, 'Hello my name is Paul, and I'm looking for some voluntary work.'

The lady told me her name and said, 'The best person to speak to is my husband; he's out at the moment, but when he comes home I will get him to phone you.' I handed over a copy of my CV and went home.

After about three weeks. I gave up all hope of them getting back in touch. I figured it had to be the Crohn's! A couple of days later, my mate came round with a business card. It was a charity which helped people find voluntary work. I got in contact with them and made an appointment for an interview.

The day before the interview, I planned the best bus route to take. The buses were every ten minutes, so I was going to leave about half an hour early just in case there was any hold-up; I didn't want to be late.

I arrived about twenty-five minutes early, so I sat and read my book for a while. When the lady called me into the room, we introduced our selves. Things were going well; we had a nice chat, and she was writing things down. Then I admitted, 'I am not 100 per cent reliable.'

'That's okay, we'll be able to find you something.'

Then like an idiot, I said, 'I have Crohn's Disease.' This is when her manner changed towards me. She slammed the heavy folder in which she was writing, the noise echoing in my ears. I tilted my head to look at the lady behind her daunting desk. As we made eye contact, her eyes pierced through mine like red hot lasers. My heart sunk, and my guts churned with nerves. Then my legs went to jelly; they felt more like eels than a pair of limbs.

'Thank you, Mr Davies, we will be in touch.' She made me feel dirty and worthless as a human being, and this really hurt me. I had Crohn's Disease—this didn't mean I was immune from hurt.

As I went to stand up, I felt something run down my leg. Oh no, I wasn't able to hold it! This was how she made me feel. I walked out and over to the bus stop. Looking back now, I don't know how or where I got the strength and courage to make it to the bus stop, but I did.

As the bus pulled up, it was packed with people. My knees started to tremble again, and my heart was beating faster and faster. I was so scared, and then my adrenalin started to pump. I stood there for a few seconds, though it felt like a lifetime. My brain was whizzing round, and a voice was saying, 'Don't get on.' In the end I had no choice—it was the only way home!

I found an empty seat and sat down. As I looked around at all the passengers on the bus, they were all gawping, and whispering to each other about me. I felt very uncomfortable and wanted the ground to swallow me up.

When I finely made it back to my flat, my hands were shaking as I tried to put the key in the door. When I got in, I kicked the door shut and fell in a heap. It took about half an hour to calm down and get up off the hall carpet. I went to the bathroom to get cleaned up, and my bottom half was clean—I didn't understand. It took a while to realise it was a panic attack.

The steroids which I took could sometimes make me sweat a little. That sweat must have been what I felt on my legs. It was too late, though—by now my confidence had been shattered into a million pieces.

Over the next five months I went out less and less; I even stopped going food shopping, letting my dad do it for me. I don't know what I would have done without my parents helping me out.

On the 18 December 2009, I had a really shitty day. I'd been in bed all day, and about nine fifteen in the evening, I crawled out of bed and into the kitchen. I had no fight left in me and just couldn't take any more pain and punishment. I got all the paracetamol out of the cupboard and four bottles of amitriptyline, and I crawled into the front room.

After opening all the bottles, I downed the first one and put it on the table. I sat there for a few minutes, and the pain went from moderate to severe; it was mainly in the middle of my stomach, so I went to the toilet. After about ten minutes, I crawled back into the lounge and sat on the floor in front of the Christmas tree, when all of a sudden I got a vision of my daughter. She was sitting in front of the tree with a present on her knee, and her eyes filled up with tears, which dripped onto the present. The only thing she wanted for Christmas was her dad—but he had taken an overdose and died.

At this point I had tears rolling down my cheeks. I placed the tops back on the three bottles that were left and thought about what I was doing. I couldn't do it. Chloe meant too much to me. I got in bed and sobbed myself to sleep. I had a very strange dream about cannabis, and when I came round in the morning, I felt a little bit better, so I got up and thought all day about buying some cannabis. About five o'clock I made a phone call, and by six o'clock I was stoned.

Part Four

My Experience with Cannabis

This last section is how my life changed dramatically, what I did over the months while smoking cannabis. It also includes why I decided to stop smoking.

I had just spoken to the dealer who supplied me with my cannabis. I gave the dealer my money for a quarter at the weekend. It was now Wednesday, and I had still not received the goods. He said he would drop it off later, that was no good to me—the pain had come back and felt like I had sat on a bomb which had just obliterated my back passage. When I felt this poorly and lethargic, I couldn't move or get out of bed, and this was where my day was heading. I felt like growing my own cannabis, I wouldn't because of Chloe, but that's how desperate I was.

The pain on that particular day had got so bad that I sat sobbing and rolling the floor in agony. The next thing I knew the doorbell rang. I found it difficult to get up but managed it eventually. Before answering the door, I had a quick look at myself in the mirror, and my eyes were very red and puffed up, due to my tears of pain.

I put the Humira, which had just been delivered, into my fridge. Doctors prescribed the Humira to help control the Crohn's, and it did help some, but I still suffered!

I had an accident the night before, the first time in months. I had opened my eyes, and the first thing I had noticed was the horrific smell of crap! The smell had been so bad that my eyes almost started to water. I got out of bed, and my pad was full to capacity. Fortunately none of it went on the covers, so my bed was clean.

I had to run a bath at four thirty in the morning so I could get rid of the lingering smell. When I was dry I got back into bed and thought to myself, 'I can't go back to that life—getting up two, three, or more times a night.' My stomach felt like the inside of a washing machine, with all the diarrhoea swishing around. It didn't help that I had run out of cannabis. One of the positive sides to smoking cannabis for me was it dried up the diarrhoea.

My daughter and her friend walked through the door after being at school all day. Chloe asked me if I had been crying, and I lied and said no, it was my hay fever. I did suffer from it, but not till later in the year. I phoned my mum to ask her to come round and pick Chloe up, so she could make her tea and stay the night. It usually took three to four days till I got back on my feet. My mum helps me all the time, making sure Chloe has tea and sandwiches for school.

To help the pain in my back, I had been using Cinchocaine and prednisolone, creams which had been designed to be put inside the back passage. I was still sore, but it had taken off the edge. Just then the doorbell rang—it was the dealer. He handed me the bag of cannabis and said, 'Sorry, mate. There have been a few warehouses that have been raided by the police, so there's a shortage at the moment.'

I got my tray from the kitchen and skinned up, inhaling the smoke. My body became very light, and I felt like I was hovering over the sofa. It didn't take long for the pain to leave; I lay back on my brown leather sofa and started to think about what the dealer had been saying, about the police and the raids. I'd not been able to get hold of any weed for a while, and I'd been in so much pain all day. Down the road the police were destroying all that cannabis. At the time I didn't know the true implications behind smoking and felt it was very unfair—I'd suffered all day when I could have had it.

Over the next few months I had no symptoms, and life was going well. My life still was changing, though—all I seemed to be doing was getting stoned on cannabis. As soon as I would wake up in the morning, the first thing I did was skin up. At the time the side effects were still only good; the diarrhoea and pain had gone completely.

About two weeks later, I phoned the incontinent nurse to order some pads. I got through to someone and asked if I could put an order in for Friday. The lady to whom I spoke started to laugh at the fact that I needed to wear pads. She fell about laughing so much that she had to put me through to someone else. I was put through to another lady who also found it hilarious. Inside I started to cry, and I couldn't believe that one human could treat another like this.

The thing that upset me the most was I'd been using pads for about seven years now, and I had been to the incontinent clinic to see the nurses on several occasions. Then after all these years they started to take the piss out of me—why, I didn't know. I put the phone down and sat there devastated.

A week later I decided to take Chloe to get a takeaway for her tea. It was a Sunday evening, and I'd been smoking all day, so I was quite stoned at this point. We ordered our food and paid and sat down to wait for it. I looked at the receipt and noticed I had been charged double for the food, so I walked to the counter to show the lad what had happened. He looked at the receipt and said it was right, and then he showed me that they hadn't double charged, but when I looked all I could see were two rounds of money, which had been taken of my bank card. I got the meal and went home.

It started to feel more like being on drugs than being on a medication. I had to make sure I had the money for my next fix, and when I did get the cannabis, I felt like I'd been ripped off by the dealer. All the nice feelings of smoking were starting to wear off; my body didn't feel warm and cosy anymore. I started to feel scared of going out, and when I did go I had people watching me and then following me home. I'd go round my flat checking all the doors were locked and the blinds were shut.

Of all the things I had suffered over the years, being paranoid had to be the worst. It felt like I had a black cloud wrapped round me, squeezing me tighter and tighter till I couldn't breathe. It really was a frightening time for me. Looking back now all the things that had happened were in my mind—the nurse laughing and the lad in the takeaway were paranoia.

I didn't know where to turn; did I go to see my GP, or would he blame it all on me for smoking drugs? I felt stupid getting involved with it in the first place. Each day I was becoming more and more paranoid, but instead of cutting down, I was smoking more than ever. You might think to yourself, 'Why the hell didn't you stop months ago?' Even though I had all this paranoia, I couldn't stop—I had become addicted.

I can now see why the police are so concerned about the cultivation of cannabis and its distribution. I was desperate when I first started and didn't know the true extent of what could happen to me mentally. A lot of people say it's not addictive, but it is, trust me. It's pleasant those first few months, with the feeling of warmth and happiness. Then the devil shows his true colours. I was very lucky and managed to quit, but it wasn't easy.

After Stopping Cannabis

I'd been waiting for years to take my daughter on a cruise, so at the end of August my mum, dad, Chloe, and I went on a seven-day cruise on P&O *Oriana*. It was not the newest ship in the fleet, but she was beautiful and classy; I'd recommend her to anyone.

A few days before we went, I had my last joint. I knew full well I couldn't take any with me, so the consultant put my steroids up, while we were away, enabling me to eat little bits of food, which was out of this would. I'd love to go back on her one day.

It's now the middle of September 2010, and I've still not had any cannabis since I quit before going on holiday. I'm really pleased with myself; it's been hard but I'm getting there.

I had a rude awakening this morning: as I turned over in my bed, my stomach felt very hard and swollen. I got up and made myself a brew and put the television on, watching it for about an hour. When I have pain like this, I find it hard to go to the toilet. I tried going and sat there for twenty minutes pushing but had no luck. When I get pain that bad, I have a very hot bath—and usually a fat joint, which eases the pain more or less straight away, but I was off cannabis. I got in the bath without the joint and soaked for an hour, which helped while I was in there.

I have a bean bag which I heat up in the microwave and put over my stomach, lying on the sofa most of the day. If it wasn't for my mum and dad helping me out with Chloe when they can, I don't know what I would do; it's not fair to Chloe when I lay down all day. Chloe lives with me, so she does spend a lot of time at home and does see me ill. I really hate that, but that's life, and we both deal with it as best we can.

She is twelve now and is able to help me with things like vacuuming and shopping. One of the sweetest things that she will do is when I'm ill, she makes sure that I am okay by asking if I need anything, and she will go get it for me, whatever it is. On my good days I really stretch my neck out to make sure I do the best I can for her.

The Middle of November

I have had a really bad week, with very bad diarrhoea and lots of pain. The pain feels like a million maggots munching their way through my stomach. My back passage, bottom, and penis have been sore with ulcers. I find when I have had a really bad week or two, the skin on the end of my thumbs starts to split and bleed. I have some hand cream which helps some, but they are still sore. It's amazing just how much you depend on your thumbs—simple things like fastening buttons on my jeans is hard to do. I do try to keep them as dry as possible, but it's easier said than done. My mood has been low; I think it's unhappy rather than being depressed, because when I start to feel a bit better, my mood will be good.

30 November

I have been to the hospital to see the consultant in outpatient today. When I went into see the consultant, he seemed to be a nice doctor, but I felt so poorly that the room was spinning and everything he said was echoing around. He said I could take the steroids up from twenty-five milligrams to thirty, but thirty is the dose I'm taking at the moment anyway; this was what the professor and I agreed on about six months ago, to keep my symptoms under control. It does control the symptoms most of the time, but at the moment the dose isn't quite high enough. He felt my stomach, which at the time was not too bad. As I sat there, I did think that I was going to be sick all over him—my mouth started to water, and the room spun. When the doctor finished speaking, he asked, 'Is there anything you want to ask me?'

'No, thank you.' I actually had a lot I wanted to ask, but I needed to get out of the room as quickly as possible. I'd been given a blood sheet to go and have some blood work done, but it was about five o'clock, and they closed at four thirty, so I needed to come back another day.

When I got home about six o'clock, I collapsed on my bed and didn't wake up till diner time the next day. I still felt ill when I woke up, but I decided to get up and watch some TV for a bit. Then around six I got back into bed till the morning.

I had a good night and felt a lot better, so when the afternoon came round, I was back in form and had a long soak in the bath. I got ready for my blood test at the hospital. I felt it was a bit of a waste of time going, because nothing would probably show up due to my feeling a lot better.

In a few days I'll be in the same boat as I was a week and go, downhill again. This happened a few months ago; I'd had a really bad time, so on the day I felt a bit better, I went to A and E, and the doctor on duty checked me all over and asked lots of questions. However, because my stomach was soft and okay, there wasn't much they could do. The doctor asked how bad the pain had been; one was okay, and ten was the worst pain ever. I said it was about a nine, and the way she looked at me said it all—I don't think she believed me. I told her about my bottom and back passage, which was sore, and she said, 'It's the pills' without even looking. I went home, and a few days later it all started again.

Over the past four years I have had two barium meals, and on both occasions I was too ill on the day, so I had to cancel till I felt better. Nothing showed up on the X-ray on both occasions, so it is hard to try and convince the doctors that there's something wrong with you when the tests are negative. It's a shame I don't know anyone else with Crohn's Disease and what their experiences have been; I can only go off of my own experience.

Sunday, 5 December 2010

I felt better till Sunday morning. I woke up, and the horrific smell in the room was unbearable, even for me. My bottom was so sore that it felt like a hot poker had been rammed into my back passage. When I got to the bathroom and took the pad off, it was overflowing, and then the smell came steaming up to my nostrils. My mouth started to water, and the sick came flowing out of me like a waterfall. I cleaned myself up and started running a bath. Before I got in, I needed the toilet, and it felt like acid coming out of me. This was the first time I ever screamed out in pain. When I got in the bath, it stung for a minute or two, and then the hot water helped soothe the pain.

Over the next couple of days there was no change, so on Wednesday afternoon I made an appointment with the GP. Unfortunately my doctor, whom I have been with for the last ten years, was on holiday, so the only doctor I could see was a lady. I told her what had been going on, and she had a look at my penis, which for the first time in a long time was very sore and scabby, and it looked very unsavoury. This didn't faze me in the slightest, and I did not feel like a freak. She prescribed some cream and bumped my steroids up to forty milligrams. She said, 'I will write to the hospital to see if they can help.' I was happy with that and had to go back in a week to see her.

On Friday I felt a lot better. It was Chloe's turn—she didn't feel too well and stayed home from school. She was supposed to see her mum that night, but I'd have to decide later depending on how she feels.

I couldn't believe it was the tenth of December already—I'd not even started Christmas shopping for Chloe yet! What was difficult was trying to think of what to buy for her. I asked her, but she couldn't decide, so it will probably be last-minute shopping again. It seemed to happen every year, and I hated it. It was my own fault; I should have been more organised. Next year maybe I would start in January.

On Friday I had a brilliant day. I got all my washing done and dried in the day, only because that week I had a new tumble drier delivered. I'd been so ill that this was the first opportunity I had to use it. This was going to be a real help to me; it sometimes took two days for some things to dry on their own, and I wouldn't have to sort the washing out and lay it out on to the washing line and radiators now.

Chloe had just come home from her mums; she seemed to be a bit better this afternoon, so I let her go. She had only been back ten minutes and said to me, 'Dad, how can you feel so poorly one minute and so well the next?' I thought about it but had no answer for her; it was hard to explain.

Friday, 17 December 2010

It has been a year since that dreadful night, and I feel so much more alive than this day last year. I have also had some good news from the hospital this morning. The blood test I had a few weeks ago has shown active Crohn's, so I can increase my Humira from every two weeks to ever ten days, so hopefully it will control things better. At the moment I'm okay and hope I stay well for Christmas and the new year.

It's 22 December, and I have been out Christmas shopping. Chloe has decided to have a phone, which me and her mum bought on Sunday. I went to a card shop this afternoon to purchase a box for a bracelet I've got for her, and as I looked round the shop, I spotted a money box with her name on it. There were two shades of pink, and I chose the darker pink for her. The queue was unbelievably long. As I got to the front of the queue, I had a quick glance at the money box one more time just before paying for it. I saw that I had picked the wrong one up—it said Claire instead of Chloe on it. I got the right one in the end, though I had to wait even longer.

It is one of those money boxes with no way to get the money out, unless you smash it. So just before wrapping it, I placed a pound into the box. Every so often I'll throw a few quid into it. Then on her twenty-first birthday, she can smash it. I can't wait to give it to her; she will go mad over the years, wanting to get her hands on the money.

Saturday, 25 December 2010

I opened my eyes very slowly and came round nice and slow. As I got out of bed, I rummaged about in the dark, looking for my phone on the floor. It was nowhere to be seen, so as I walked to put the light on, I stubbed my toe on the corner of the bed. I finally found the phone and looked at the time—five thirty. I didn't have to be up till seven o'clock, so I went back to bed for an hour or so.

The next thing I knew it was eight o'clock, and I jumped up ut of bed and phoned the ex wife, who was picking me up at eight. When I got through she was still in bed too. I'm just glad I'd gone back to bed for a bit, otherwise I would have been waiting. She arranged to pick me up at nine o'clock.

I decided to have a bath just before I went to my mum's for dinner. I had a wash and a shave, and looking in the mirror got me thinking about last year, about my attempting to overdose. All the memories came flooding back. Seeing Chloe there on Christmas day in front of the tree, crying and wishing. This brought a tear to my eye, just thinking about how easily I could have died; if I had of just drunk some more, I wouldn't be stood here now. I put the razor down and prayed to God, thanking him for the things he had given to me, the positive and the negative. I believed things happen for a reason, and the negative parts of my life were there to help me learn and make me stronger.

There are some things in life that people can say and do which make life worth living and can keep you going. Chloe said to me a few days after Christmas, 'Dad, I've got some Christmas money. Instead of a present for myself, I'd like to take you out shopping, so I can buy you something to say thank you for all the lovely presents you have brought for me.' This almost broke my heart in two. No matter how much I have been through, how much it smells when I go to the toilet, and the things I've done, she still loves me with all her heart. I am the luckiest man in the world, to have such a lovely little girl. Chloe is twelve now, but she will always be my little girl.

When I was ready, I went round to Molly's to see Chloe open her presents from her mum and that side of the family. After Chloe opened all her presents, we came back to my flat so she could open the presents from me and my family. We have done it this way for the past four years; it saves any arguments, and we both get to see her open everything everyone has bought for her.

At eleven thirty Molly went to have her Christmas dinner with her friend. When she had gone, I helped Chloe with her new phone, which I'd brought for her.

At three o'clock my brother-in-law picked Chloe and me up, and he took us to my mum's for Christmas dinner. We go there every year for our dinner with my sister and her two girls. I don't ever eat except on holidays or Christmas, and I always end up regretting it, but it smelt too good to resist, so I had two potatoes, two sausages, and some carrots. This was about four o'clock. By five thirty I was in so much pain it was unbelievable, so at six I had to go home. You'd think I'd have learnt by now.

New Year's, 2011

I have almost finished writing my book, I have learnt so much the last year. The one thing that has gotten me through the past few months without the use of cannabis is my book. I love writing so much now and am really looking forward to finishing my novel. The most important thing is to stay positive and never give up, because good days will come!